This Book is Gratefully Dedicated to All My Clients

"Radio Advertising Does Not Work." Says Who?
What You Need to Know about Radio Advertising
www.RadioAdvertisingBook.com

Published by American Mass Media Corporation
SAN 850–9654
207 East Ohio Street, Suite 218,
Chicago, IL 60611, USA

Library of Congress Control Number (LCCN)
2006903519

ISBN 0-9785597-0-3

To My Clients

Dear Clients,

Thank you for your business all these years! You've taught me much about advertising, business and life. You have shown me how to apply the strengths of radio to your business. You have voted for radio with your hard-earned money. You are the true believers in radio advertising.

Sincerely,

The Author

The Use of the
Male Singular Pronoun

To avoid the composition of cumbersome sentences caused by the use of "he or she," throughout this book the male singular pronoun "he" will be used for the singular third person. Any suggestion of sexual discrimination is rejected in advance.

Contents

Chapter 1

Do You Need to Advertise?

Chapter 1

Do You Need to Advertise?

Selling is a numbers game. The more potential customers you reach, the more likely you will find the next customer.

Advertising is mass selling. In fact, David Ogilvy called advertising "the cheapest form of selling." Advertising helps you reach more people more efficiently, thereby improving the odds on reaching your next customer.

Is your business ready to mass sell? The following questionnaire will help you find out.

Do the following statements describe your business?

		Yes	No
1.	I am receptive to advertising.	_	_
2.	My staff is receptive to advertising.	_	_
3.	I have a good product or service.	_	_
4.	I have a unique offer.	_	_
5.	I will sell more if more people know about my offer.	_	_
6.	People don't think of my company when they need my product or service.	_	_

3

7. People don't know about my web site. _ _

8. I want to increase market share. _ _

9. My offer is better than those of my competitors. _ _

10. I want to expand my company. _ _

11. I want my company to be an industry leader. _ _

12. My industry is competitive. _ _

13. My business is relationship-driven. _ _

14. I need a steady stream of new customers. _ _

15. I want my potential customers to buy *sooner*. _ _

16. I want my customers to buy *again*. _ _

17. My salespeople make cold calls by phone or in person. _ _

18. I'd rather that my salespeople spend their time on closing business than on cold calling. _ _

19. My potential customers are skeptical about my offers. _ _

20. My potential customers don't respect my salespeople. _ _

21. My salespeople don't speak with confidence. _ _

22. My employees don't feel proud of their company. _ _

23. I want to hire talented people. _ _

24. I want to retain good employees.   _ _
25. I want to ride the booms longer.   _ _
26. I want to recover from recessions sooner.   _ _
27. I want to attract investors.   _ _

Total: = =

Yes answers 0-9:
There's no urgency to advertise. Advertising should be considered on an as-needed basis only.

Yes answers 10-18:
Advertising is recommended to speed up your company's growth. Allocate a small to mid-size budget and start weighing your options.

Yes answers 19-27:
Advertising is essential to your survival. It is the bread and butter of your business. Allocate a sizeable budget, weigh your options, and advertise.

Mark Twain wrote, "Many a small thing has been made large by the right kind of advertising." This book is written to help you understand one kind of advertising that's widely-used but little-understood, *radio*, so that you will determine if it is the right kind of advertising for your business.

Chapter 2

When to Advertise on Radio

Chapter 2

When to Advertise on Radio

There's no medium like radio. An average household owns five to six radios. Radio is in the bedroom, living room, basement, bathroom, kitchen and garage. Radio is in the workplace. Radio is in the car. Radio is also on the Internet.

Best of all, radio is free, and almost everybody listens to it. According to the Radio Advertising Bureau (RAB), radio reaches 93% of consumers each week! In other words, 228,910,000 listeners across the United States tune to radio each week!

Recognizing the pervasiveness of radio, advertisers invested more than $21 *b*illion in radio in 2005!

So, let us look at when and how you may best use this pervasive medium, and the logic behind it all.

1. If your business is relationship-driven, advertise on radio.

JC Penny said, "Every business is built on friendship." And radio has the power to befriend. Listening to radio is a personal experience, not a group one.

9

The best radio hosts understand the intimate nature of this medium, and are skillful at creating the illusion that each listener is the only person they're speaking to.

To be successful in radio advertising, you must *not* treat radio as a mass medium. Make your message personal so as to connect with your listeners one-to-one. Words like "you" and "I" are more engaging on radio than "the customers," "our company," "you folks," or "all of you." On radio, you're not talking to an auditorium of consumers. You're speaking to a friend, one-to-one.

2. If your potential customers are difficult-to-reach, advertise on radio.

Radio is the only medium that reaches people everywhere in almost any circumstances.

Just think. When was the last time you learned of a thunderstorm from billboards? Woke up to the sound of direct mail? Watched TV while jogging? Looked up the Yellow Pages on the beach? Surfed the Internet at a tailgate party? Read the newspaper while driving? Or enjoyed a magazine in the dark?

You can do all of the above with radio.

Radio is like a salesman in your potential customers' cars, kitchens, bedrooms or workplaces; it allows you to sell even when you are not in front of them.

3. If you want to build customer loyalty, advertise on radio.

Radio listeners are loyal to their stations. Each listener stays loyal to only two to three stations. This is true even in large markets like New York, Los Angeles and Chicago where there are 30 to 40 radio signals!

People's choice of stations reflects who they are; it is deeply personal. Listeners find it as enjoyable to listen to their favorite station as it is unpleasant to listen to one that they don't care for!

Furthermore, listeners stay with their stations for years. Many stations have a multi-generational following. Their listeners grew up listening to their parents' station; and now they are listening to the same station with their own children.

Furthermore, listeners share a kinship with one another. It is a delight to meet someone who also listens to your station. Conversely, it is disagreeable to hear criticisms of your station.

Such is the loyalty that listeners have toward their stations; and you can transfer some of that loyalty to your business by

- voicing over your own commercials to speak one-to-one to your listeners;

- hiring a radio host to endorse your business;

- hiring a radio host to read your copy *live* (instead of pre-recording it);

- hiring a radio station to broadcast live from your place of business;

- sponsoring a station event.

4. If you know your customers, advertise on the radio station whose audience most resembles them.

Radio is highly targetable. Different formats attract different demographics and psychographics. Most radio stations have access to media researches such as those provided by Arbitron, Scarborough and Media Audit. Your radio stations are, therefore, able to show you a great deal of information about their listeners including their age, homeownership, brands of vehicles, income levels, types of employment, as well as education.

You can also learn a lot about a station from its *long-term advertisers*. Ask the stations for a list of advertisers who have been on their air for more than two years. Then ask yourself, "Who are *their* customers?" For example, if a station has many long-term advertisers selling luxury cars, investment products and vacation homes, you can safely assume that this station has an affluent, perhaps older, audience.

5. If you sell to upper-income individuals, you must advertise on radio.

Radio is particularly adept at reaching the elusive upper-income individuals. In general, formats such as All-News, Talk, Classical Music and National Public Radio attract the affluent and educated. There are exceptions, of course, but start your search with these stations.

6. If you want to be cost-effective, advertise on radio.

Radio is under-priced. Compared to TV, newspapers, magazines and direct mail, radio offers the lowest Cost per Thousand (CPM). With radio, you can reach a person several times over for pennies! Not only that, radio's advertising rates are not increasing as quickly as those of other media.

But the real bargains come from the following opportunities:

Non-Prime Times. Evenings and overnights are disproportionately under-priced, thanks to the misconception that nobody listens to radio at night. The truth is that many stations attract a loyal nighttime audience of tens of thousands! In fact, it is at night that 50,000-watt stations are heard in numerous states!

First and Third Quarters. Also under-priced are certain months of the year, particularly January, February, July and August. During these months, a moderate budget can finance a strong campaign.

Holidays. And then there are the public holidays (Fourth of July, Thanksgiving Day, Christmas Day, New Year's Day…etc), as well as weekends. You can get rock-bottom rates on these days, and dominate your station all day long.

New Formats. Whenever there's a new station, you can expect to get rock-bottom pricing. Most new stations virtually give themselves away in an effort to build relationships with advertisers and create success stories. So be on the lookout for new radio stations. If a new station's target audience is a good enough match for your business, buy as many commercials for as little money as you can get away with.

Buying in Advance. If you book for a full year, instead of buying month to month, you will receive better offers.

However, depending on the discounts you receive, you may or may not be able to cancel your contract. But in most cases, if you have a good enough relationship with your station, it will let you cancel with as little as two weeks' notice.

Buying Cancellations. Let stations know that if they have a last-minute cancellation, you're willing to buy it at 40-50% off. Advertisers sometimes cancel at the last minute, leaving stations with unsold inventory that needs to be turned back into revenue.

7. If you want direct response, advertise on radio.

A trusted friend recommending a product or service is very persuasive. The human voice also conveys urgency better than printed words and pictures. That's why so many products and services are sold directly on radio, from vacuum cleaners, air purifiers, mattresses, diamonds and flowers to cheesecakes, ham, steaks and even lobsters; never mind insurance, mortgages, legal services, business consultations and vacation packages.

Radio generates highly-motivated leads. The reason is that it takes a lot of effort to respond to a radio commercial. People are doing something while listening to the radio (driving, cleaning, cooking, jogging...etc). They have to drop whatever they're doing to write down your phone number and call you. They certainly don't do that to waste their own time.

To get a direct response, the prime incentive is the promise of a benefit. And to improve direct response, the radio commercial must end with a phone number spoken three times in succession at dictation speed.

8. If you need to change your commercials frequently, radio allows you to do it cost-effectively.

Radio production is simple, quick and very affordable. In most cases, your radio station will produce the entire commercial (from writing to recording) for no extra charge. Many stations house a music and sound-effects library. These stations' BMI-ASCAP license may allow you free use of copyrighted materials in your commercials. For an affordable fee, most stations can arrange for actors to perform dramatic voice-overs.

Radio's flexible and affordable production makes this medium a natural choice for certain advertisers. For example, my station's mortgage advertisers frequently update their commercials to reflect the changes in interest rates. Manufacturers of emergency power generators and backup sump pumps adjust their commercials according to weather conditions. Carpet cleaning and disaster restoration companies refer to specific floods that have occurred. On one occasion, the workers of a large pharmacy went on strike. Its competitors quickly changed their radio messages to capitalize on the situation. Most interestingly, a clinic that offers coronary screening revises its commercial whenever a famous person dies of heart failure to remind listeners of the importance of advance screening.

9. If you have a web site, advertise it on radio.

Dot-com companies embrace radio, taking advantage of the fact that radio listeners are heavy Internet users. A variety of dot-com campaigns can be heard on radio, including those for search engines, auctions, dating services, travel, education, real estate and retail goods. These dot-com advertisers often see an immediate increase in web hits within seconds of a radio commercial.

Radio and the Internet complement each other. The former is persuasive; the latter is informative. Radio piques the curiosity; the Internet satisfies it. Radio tells a story with sound; the Internet confirms it with words and pictures. Radio is intrusive and free; the Internet is easily accessible and affordable. Radio generates leads; the web site takes the orders. Both are targetable, interactive and immediate.

It is fascinating how one of the oldest media works so well with one of the newest!

10. If you advertise on TV, add radio.

Radio brings back images of TV commercials to people's minds, an effect called *Imagery Transfer*. Radio, with its low CPM, is an affordable medium to increase the frequency, reach and longevity of your TV campaign.

To produce a TV commercial is time-consuming and costly. But radio production is fast and affordable so that frequent copy updates are possible.

Radio picks up where TV leaves off. While TV reaches most households at night at home, radio reaches most individuals during the day when they are outside. Radio is, therefore, closer to the point of purchase than TV.

Moreover, certain radio stations (e.g., All-News, Talk, and Classical Music) reach the upper-income people very effectively because they tend to be light TV viewers.

Radio not only complements TV but it also offers event marketing and promotions, which are almost never offered by TV stations and cable companies.

11. If you advertise in newspapers, add radio.

Newspapers are a good resource for price and feature comparisons, and an effective medium to reach consumers who are actively seeking information about a product or service.

The problem is that if your newspaper advertisement is next to your competitor's and your offers are similar, how are you going to draw attention to *your* advertisement?

Add radio.

Radio is "in your face." It seeks out potential customers and pre-sells your product or service to them.

Radio also has the ability to befriend. If your offer is similar to your competitors', then the friendship you build through radio will give you an added advantage.

In addition, radio reaches light readers and non-readers, especially people under thirty-five, thereby opening new markets for you.

Newspaper advertisements can be shrunk in size with little loss of readership. The savings can then be re-allocated to radio, increasing the reach and frequency of your advertising.

When you have advertisements both in the newspapers and on radio, be sure to cross-reference them. Print in your newspaper advertisement "As heard on

WBBB," and mention in your radio commercial "See our ad in this Sunday's papers." This way, you will reap a bigger harvest.

12. If you advertise in the Yellow Pages, add radio.

The Yellow Pages are an excellent reference tool. Like newspapers, the Yellow Pages reach people who are making the purchase decision.

However, what if your advertisement is surrounded by your competitors'? How can you make yours stand out?

Add radio.

Lane Kirkland said, "Go where the customer is and don't expect him to come to you. The only way to convert a heathen is to travel into the jungle." The Yellow Pages are passive but radio is "in your face;" it takes your offer to your potential customers instead of waiting for them to come to you.

The Yellow Pages are closed most of the time whereas radio reaches 93% of consumers every week. In addition, because the Yellow Pages are published only once a year, your advertisement cannot be changed for that period. Radio, on the other hand, is real-time and flexible. Radio commercials are frequently updated to be relevant to their listeners' lives.

Most important, radio announcers transfer audience loyalty to your brand, compensating for the impersonality of Yellow Pages. Like radar, radio constantly scans for prospective customers; like a friend, it recommends your company so that when those listeners turn to the Yellow Pages, it is your name that they will seek out. To take advantage of the synergy between radio and Yellow Pages, make sure you mention in your commercial, *Find us in the Yellow Pages.*"

13. If you advertise in magazines, add radio.

The two similarities between magazines and radio are targetability and portability. Both media reach targeted groups; and both can be enjoyed almost anywhere. When you add a matching radio audience to your magazine readership, you increase the reach and frequency of your advertising.

Radio also directs attention to your magazine advertisement. Radio sells with a human voice. Magazine sells with pictures and words. Radio adds a human element to the visual display in your magazine advertisement.

Radio broadcasts live; magazines are published periodically. Adding radio to your advertising mix creates a greater sense of urgency to purchase. Most important, radio reaches the non-readers of the magazine, whom you would otherwise miss.

14. If you use direct mail, add radio.

Direct mail can target with precision. It is especially effective when used to target people about whom information has been previously collected.

Direct mail is tangible. It is also more detailed than radio. To many consumers, seeing an offer in writing gives them reassurance.

Direct mail is not cheap, however. It has a significantly higher CPM than radio. To make matters worse, much direct mail is considered junk and thrown away unopened. So how do you get the most out of your direct mail?

Add radio.

People tend to open mail from people they know. Radio's ability to befriend turns junk mail into friendly mail.

Moreover, by adding radio, you bring down your overall CPM while increasing reach and frequency. It's a win-win situation.

15. If you have salespeople, support them with radio.

Paradoxically, radio is personal selling *en masse*. Instead of speaking to one potential customer at a time as in personal selling, radio enables you to speak to thousands of them all at once; and each one of this mass audience feels that he is being addressed personally.

For the cost of hiring an additional salesman, you should "hire" a radio station to mass sell for you. Think of your radio station as a good salesman. In fact, this salesman is so good that he has the power to befriend, turn cold calls into warm calls, and build loyalty so that each week hundreds of thousands listen.

Use radio to sow the seeds. Let your salespeople reap the harvest.

16. If you use outdoor advertising, add radio.

In large metropolitan areas, outdoor displays such as billboards on highways, signage at airports, and posters on buses, are visible to hundreds of thousands of consumers!

Outdoor advertising is an excellent image builder. It showcases your brand, creating awareness and reinforcing recognition. Outdoor advertising also generates direct response; it's often used to direct potential customers to retail locations.

However, outdoor advertising is as good as its location; and good locations are not cheap. A client of mine pays $30,000 a month to display his billboard (yes, only one billboard) by a major highway! Although he is not sure how much revenue the billboard has generated, he loves the visibility which is important to many businesses.

To get the most out of your outdoor advertising, add radio. Radio reaches more of your potential customers more often - both indoors and outdoors. Furthermore, radio turns your brand into a familiar name, making your outdoor advertising more recognizable. Moreover, radio reaches millions of commuters each week and is, therefore, an ideal medium to reinforce your outdoor advertising.

17. If you do event marketing, involve a radio station.

If you think that radio advertising is about buying air time, think again. Radio is also about event marketing. In fact, many stations rely on it for revenue.

Radio stations are very involved in their communities. At almost every major event, there's an official radio station. Radio stations offer contests, giveaways, and celebrity appearances; they can add great excitement to an event. My clients, through my station's connections, have had their logos displayed and products sampled at football games and golf tournaments. But it was the attention my station brought to their displays that was invaluable. My clients' booths were crowded!

Each time you are to put together a sizeable event or to be part of one (be it a job fair, golf tournament, business luncheon, or home-remodeling expo), partner with a radio station, especially with a station on which you're already advertising.

18. If you want to influence the influencers, advertise on radio.

No man is an island. We don't make decisions alone. We are constantly influenced by the people in our lives. Have you never talked to a family member when considering a large purchase? Have you not bought something because your friends had it? Don't neighbors get home-improvement ideas from one another? Generally speaking, the larger the purchase, the more people we ask.

For that reason, as an advertiser, it is important to look beyond your immediate potential customers to those who influence them.

Spreading the word among friends is what radio does cost-effectively. Radio is precise enough to target your potential customers, but also broad enough to reach those who influence them. Like a trusted friend spreading good news, radio is the ultimate word-of-mouth medium.

19. If you sell visual products, advertise them on radio.

Many of my clients advertise exclusively on radio. Yet, their customers have reported seeing them on TV! What's going on?

Radio is the theatre of the mind.

Charles Osgood often says, "I'll see you on the radio." He means that you will see him in your mind's eye when you hear him.

This emphasizes the misconception that radio is TV without pictures. The truth is that radio is TV with *better* pictures. As Osgood points out, "They haven't come out with a TV screen big enough, bright, clear, and colorful enough to equal the capacity of the mind to create [one's] own vivid images." Sometimes the most striking pictures are the ones we cannot see.

Radio evokes a visual response and sells visual products effectively. In fact, most products sold on radio are appreciated visually. Examples are automobiles, furniture, real estate, vacation destinations, jewelry, gifts, clothes, cameras, flowers, books…just to name the obvious few.

What creates radio's visual quality is good writing and good announcing. The best radio copywriters compose not just for the ear but also for the eye. The most talented announcers are very expressive; they use facial expressions and body language as if performing on stage. With the aid of music and sound effects, radio paints as vivid a picture as human imagination allows.

Chapter 3

How to Measure Your Return on Radio Advertising

Chapter 3

How to Measure Your Return on Radio Advertising

Advertising is an investment and a calculated risk. Before you invest in radio advertising, ask yourself, "What do I want out of it?" Set a quantifiable goal: for example, 5 new customers per month; 100 phone calls per week; 200 sales per year; increasing awareness by 25%.

Too often, inexperienced advertisers simply call up all the radio stations they can think of, get prices over the phone, and choose the cheapest station with which to advertise.

Good stations are not cheap; cheap stations are not good. Asking about rates may scare you away from the very station that can help you.

Simply tell the radio stations your expectation (e.g., 100 phone calls per month). Then ask them to show you how they can meet your goal, and how much it would cost.

How to Set a Radio Budget

Step 1: Know your own numbers.

In order to set the right budget, you need to know these numbers:

- Your average profit per sale.
- The worth of a customer

Let's say your profit is $1,000 per sale, and an average customer makes 3 purchases from you over his lifetime. The worth of a customer is, therefore, $3,000. (To simplify our calculation, we will assume that your customers do not refer other customers to you.)

Step 2: Set a measurable goal.

How many new customers do you want from your radio advertising? 1 per week? 10 per month? 100 per year?

Step 3: Calculate your total potential profit.

Worth of a customer x Number of customers wanted = Total potential profit

If the worth of a customer is $3,000, and you want 100 customers, your total potential profit will be:

$3,000 x 100 customers = $300,000

Step 4: Allocate 15%-30% of your potential profit to radio advertising.

David Ogilvy wrote, "advertising is still an inexact speculation." As with any inexact speculation, the return ought to be high.

If $300,000 is your total potential profit, your radio advertising budget should be between $45,000 and $90,000.

Example 1: Shelly's Restaurant

Shelly's Restaurant wants to use radio to gain 100 new customers a year. The average profit per customer per visit is $20. An average customer patronizes the restaurant 6 times a year, and comes back for at least 3 years.

The worth of a customer:

	$20	(Average profit per visit)
x	6	(Visits per year)
x	3	(Years of patronage)
=	$360	(Worth of a customer)

Maximum potential profit from 100 customers over 3 years:

	$360	(Worth of a customer)
x	100	(Number of new customers wanted)
=	$36,000	(Maximum potential profit over 3 years)

$36,000 is the maximum potential profit Shelly's Restaurant can expect from 100 new customers. The Restaurant then decides to allocate 30% to radio advertising, that is,

$10,800. If it achieves its goal, it will make a profit of $25,200, or 233% over 3 years.

Example 2: Macau Corporation

Macau Corporation plans to launch a direct-response radio campaign. Its goal is to make 100 sales in a year. A typical sale brings $500 of profit.

Maximum potential profit from 100 sales:

	$500	(Profit per sale)
x	100	(Number of sales wanted)
=	$50,000	(Maximum potential profit)

Since $50,000 is the maximum potential profit Macau Corporation can make from 100 sales, the Corporation decides to invest 30% of it in radio advertising (i.e., $15,000). If it achieves 100 sales, it will make a profit of $35,000, or 233% in 1 year.

How Do I Know Which Customers Come From Radio?

Advertising is an inexact science and difficult to measure. Department store pioneer John Wanamaker once said, "Half the money I spend on advertising is wasted; the trouble is, I don't know which half."

To be able to measure how many customers come from radio depends on a few factors:

1. Whether you also advertise with other media
2. How strong your offer is
3. How specific your call for action is
4. How easy it is for listeners to respond

Actual Case 1:

A mortgage broker advertised refinancing with no closing cost. The business owner repeated his offer and phone number throughout his commercial. He advertised exclusively on one radio station. Each time his commercial aired, the phone rang. He knew exactly how much profit radio generated for him because that was the only medium he used.

Actual Case 2:

A restaurant had always advertised its Mother's Day Buffet in the local newspapers which had brought 1,000 customers every year. One year, the restaurant decided to add radio. 3,000 customers showed up! A record in the restaurant's 20-year history! The owner knew with a high degree of certainty how many customers came from radio.

Actual Case 3:

A high-end shoe store had always advertised its annual sale by mailing coupons to pre-selected zip codes. One year, it added radio. Its coupon redemption that year noticeably increased. The floor traffic noticeably increased. And business continued to be good even *after* the sale. In this case, although the owner could not identify which customers came in as a result of radio (because most people came in holding a coupon), he knew that radio had contributed to the higher coupon redemption.

The cash register is your best indicator.

In some cases, we can calculate the number of customers sent by radio with reasonable accuracy. In others, it's an educated guess. The best way to measure the effectiveness of any type of advertising is to monitor the changes to your cash register.

Chapter 4

7 Steps to Buying Radio Advertising

Chapter 4

7 Steps to Buying Radio Advertising

Buying radio advertising can be done systematically. Generally, there are 7 steps to it.

Step 1: Compile a Customer Profile

You are not buying a commercial. You are buying an audience. Whether you end up on the right station depends on how well you know your own customers. You need to compile a customer profile that includes the following:

- What is the socio-economic description of your customers (age, income, residence, occupation, education…etc)?
- How much is a customer worth?
- Why do they buy from you? (Price? Quality? Relationship? Location?)
- How far do they travel to come to you?
- When do they buy from you? How often?
- At how many places have they shopped before coming to you?
- How long do they take to make a decision?
- Who influences them in their decision?

List as many things as you know about your customers and keep your customer profile up-to-date.

Step 2: Compile a Business Profile

In addition to knowing your customers, you also need to know your business. Your business profile will answer the following questions:

- What is your annual revenue?
- What is your profit margin?
- Who are your competitors?
- What is unique about your business?
- What types of advertising are you using? How effective are they?
- What advertising are your competitors doing?
- What market share do you have?
- What are your short-term and long-term goals?
- What is the next opportunity for growth?
- What do you want to get out of radio advertising?

Step 3: Set a Quantifiable Goal.

After you've compiled data about your customers and business, you need to set a quantifiable goal, i.e., 10 calls per week, 50 customers a month…etc.

Step 4: Meet with Account Executives for Needs Analyses

Meeting with Account Executives from stations that you are considering is time-consuming but important.

An Account Executive's first duty is to learn about your business. He is doing his job when he asks for a face-to-face Needs Analysis. Grant him that interview. The more he knows about your business, the better a campaign he can recommend. During the meeting, the Account Executive should be asking you a lot of questions to help him learn. If any Account Executive tries to sell to you before he understands your business, stop the meeting and show him the door. He did not come to help you.

After the Needs Analysis, your Account Executive will prepare his proposal. He will ask for a second meeting to present his ideas.

Step 5: Meet with Account Executives for Proposals

The second meeting is for you to find out how each radio station can help your business and at what cost.

Your Account Executives will return with research data, ideas, offers, and sample commercials. Every station will tell you that it is number one; and it is not lying. Radio stations can be ranked in so many different ways that a station is bound to rank first one way or another by its own criteria.

"Ratings" do not mean advertising success. Time and time again, second- or third-ranking stations outperform top-rated stations in generating results. For example, a station that is top-rated at targeting women is not necessarily better than a station that targets a mixed audience if the mixed audience includes a greater number of women likely to respond to an advertisement.

During your second meetings, you will see:

- which Account Executives work in your best interest, and
- which proposals have substance.

Step 6: Eliminate, and Eliminate Some More

After listening to all the presentations, you will have a good idea which stations may be able to help your business.

Chances are that you are still left with more stations than you can afford. **To advertise with impact, it is better to focus on just one or two stations.** So, you need to eliminate some more.

Let the finalists know that you're comparing their offers. Tell them to sharpen their pencils and submit better offers. The purpose is not to look for the cheapest station to buy from but rather to *eliminate.*

The advertising rates of a station, which reflect its effectiveness, are modified by the law of supply and demand. Good stations are not cheap. Cheap stations are not good. The Account Executive who returns with the sharpest drop in price should be eliminated, for that is a tell-tale sign that his station is not effective and that he has not been forthcoming with you.

Now that you've eliminated the least impressive finalist and received better offers from the rest, you should have a very good idea which station you'd like to buy from.

But before you select the winner, spend a few days listening to it. Pay attention to the following:

- Who are its long-term advertisers?
- Whom are these advertisers trying to reach?
- How many commercials does the station run per break?
- Does the station have commercial-free hours to help listeners avoid your commercials?
- Do the hosts instill loyalty or are they controversial so that some listeners will be antagonized?

Step 7: Place your order

The final step is to place your order with the station that shows the most potential to meet your expectations.

But hold it! Before you sign on the dotted line, ask for added value. Your Account Executive may have already included added value in his proposal, but you owe it to yourself to get *more*. The following is what you should ask for:

- **Free commercials.** Radio stations routinely give away evening and overnight spots, as well as 10-second and 15-second ones. Any extra commercials will help your campaign; so ask for them.

- **Free billboards.** These are short mentions, often announced live by the radio hosts. For example, *"This program is brought to you by the Riviera Corporation, Serving the Business Community."* Radio stations routinely give these away, so make sure you get your fair share.

- **Free web listing.** It costs a radio station close to nothing to list your company name on its website; so ask for a listing on the website.

- **Free promotions.** These include anything from distributing your brochures at an event, to displaying your logo on the station vehicle, to contests and giveaways, as well as a live broadcast from your business (known as a "remote").

An effective way to get what you want is to add it to the agreement yourself, sign it, and fax it to your Account Executive. That is your official advertising order. Most Account Executives find it difficult to walk away from business that's actually in their hands.

Chapter 5

6 Components of a Successful Radio Campaign

Chapter 5

6 Components of a Successful Radio Campaign

A successful radio campaign has 6 indispensable components:

1. Target Audience (Who are your potential customers?)
2. Frequency (How often do you ask your potential customers for business?)
3. Reach (How many potential customers do you talk to?)
4. Persistence (How long have you been asking them for business?)
5. Audience Attention (How attentively are they listening to you?)
6. The Commercial Itself (What do you tell them, and how?)

1. Target Audience

Selecting which audience to advertise to is like selecting which stock to buy; it directly affects your return on investment. If 80% of your profit comes from customers 35-64 years of age with an income of $75,000, logically, you should advertise on the radio station that reaches the largest pool of people with these demographics.

Ask your stations for a *cume* ranker on the demographics that matter to your business. *Cume* is industry jargon for *cumulative persons.* It tells you how many people listen to a station. The following ranker shows the *cumes* of three stations.

Qualitative Criteria:
A35-64, Income $75,000+
Daypart: M-SU 6A-12M

STATIONS	CUME
WBBB	350,000
WMMM	200,000
WZZZ	150,000

The above ranker shows that between 6 AM and midnight between Monday and Sunday, WBBB reaches a total of 350,000 people 35-64 years of age with an income of at least $75,000.

Although WBBB reaches the largest number of your target market, it does not automatically mean that it is the station with which you should advertise. It merely means that WBBB deserves your consideration the most. After all, the second and third stations also reach sizeable audiences.

2. Frequency

Tell the listeners what you're going to tell them. Tell them. Then tell them what you've just told them. Repetition is a very important part of selling.

People don't remember things that they've heard only once. Radio needs repetition to work, preferably repetition that occurs at short intervals so that you achieve saturation. Unfortunately, not every company can afford to saturate a radio station every day and every week. A good method to create the *impression* of saturation is to narrow your schedule.

For example, one of my clients can afford only 6 prime-time commercials per week. He, therefore, narrows them to only Tuesdays and Thursdays so that on each day he airs 3 commercials. In general, **high frequency over a short period of time (vertical saturation) creates a stronger impact than low frequency over a long period of time (horizontal saturation),** although both methods have produced successful campaigns.

Another good way to supplement a light schedule is to buy a large number of "rotators." (Some stations call them *Run-*

of-Schedules, or *ROSs*.) Rotators are commercials aired at less predictable times, and are, therefore, relatively cheap. In my client's case, it costs him very little to add 10 rotators every week to air Tuesday-Saturday, 5a-12m. Although most of his rotators air at night, some do get upgraded into prime times, giving him great value for his money.

3. Reach

Selling is a numbers game. The more people you reach, the better your chances of finding the next customer.

Your *reach* is affected by (a) the *cume* of your station, (b) the frequency of your commercials; and (c) the time your commercials go on the air. You can't calculate *reach* yourself because you need rating numbers. Ask your radio stations to show you the *reach* of your campaign.

4. Persistence

Successful radio advertisers often hear their customers say, "You're on the radio all the time!" when in fact they are not. Nobody can afford that! These advertisers are merely long-term, persistent advertisers. Many of my station's most successful advertisers have been on the air for 10 to 20 years!

All of these advertisers understand that a ten-week campaign is not enough to take their businesses to the next level. But a ten-week campaign three times a year for the next five years is.

By advertising consistently over a long period of time, you reassure your potential customers that your company is stable and thriving. After all, if you plan to stay in business for a long time, why would you advertise as if you were a fly-by-night outfit? When your competitors take a break, you keep on marching.

5. Audience Attention

How people listen affects your advertising results. The same listener who switches between two stations may respond to your commercial on one station and ignore the same commercial on another. This happens when one station is a foreground format and the other is a background format.

Foreground formats include All-News, Talk and Sports stations. These formats, especially the All-News, consistently deliver results to advertisers. This is because when a listener tunes to a foreground station, he expects to listen to someone talk; he is therefore receptive to information, including commercials. However, being on a foreground station is not an automatic guarantee of success. Some foreground stations run too many commercials per break. As a result, their listeners get annoyed and tune out mentally and often literally.

If you advertise on a station that runs more than 3 minutes of commercials per break, make sure that your commercial is the first to air and is not buried in the clutter. For added publicity, have the hosts read your copy live or, better still, personally endorse you.

Background formats include all the music stations such as Contemporary Hits, Easy Listening, Rock, Country, Jazz, Oldies, etc. Listeners expect to hear music. Commercials are regarded as interruptions.

However, when a music station features strong local personalities, the line between foreground and background begins to blur. Popular personalities can have a following of hundreds of thousands. An endorsement by any of them is powerful!

Regardless of format, make sure your radio stations are pro-advertising. Incredible as it sounds, there are stations that do things to hurt their own advertisers. Do not advertise on any station that brags about "commercial-free" segments. Why should you spend thousands of dollars to advertise on a station only to hear it telling its listeners to avoid you?

6. The Commercial Itself

Good radio commercials are not easy to create. So if you are lucky enough to come up with a good commercial, you are half way to winning the battle. The next chapter will offer tips on how to create radio commercials that sell.

Chapter 6

How to Create Radio Commercials That Sell

Chapter 6

How to Create Radio Commercials That Sell

The radio commercial itself is the most powerful weapon in your armory. It can make or break your advertising campaign.

What Makes a Good Radio Commercial

Radio commercials come in different styles. Some consist of jingles; others of announcements; some are humorous; others serious; some are voiced-over by the business owners themselves; others by celebrities.

What separates a good commercial from a bad one is not how many awards it has won, but how many sales it has generated. In fact, some of the most effective radio commercials have never won any awards because they are not considered "creative" or "entertaining." Many of them are merely straight reads. They have no jingles, no funny dialogue, no celebrity endorsements. They're simple and straight forward. Yet they make the phone ring.

So what makes these commercials so effective? Before we can answer this question, we must examine how people listen and what goes on in their mind as they hear your commercial.

How People Listen

People multitask

People do not devote their full attention to any mass medium. They may be eating while reading the newspaper; talking on the phone while surfing the Internet; flipping through a magazine while watching TV.

Of all the media, radio is the easiest to multitask with. Radio is there when people are driving, working, jogging, cleaning, gardening, washing, showering, reading, cooking and eating.

That radio is conducive to multitasking means a few things to you as an advertiser:

1. The same listener will hear your commercial in different environments.
2. Your listener's attentiveness changes according to the environment that he is in.
3. Your listener has a small window of opportunity to catch your contact information.
4. If your listener takes the trouble to respond to your commercial, he is interested.

People listen sequentially

When people listen, they take in one idea at a time. On the other hand, when people *see*, they take in the whole picture all at once; going over the details is optional. That people listen sequentially means a few things to you as an advertiser:

1. To orally communicate a sequence of ideas takes time.
2. People can remember only a small number of ideas each time.
3. When listening, people remember ideas, not words.
4. Lists, addresses and numbers are difficult to remember.
5. Repetition helps the memory.
6. If people don't understand what you're trying to sell, they tune you out.
7. If people don't think that your message applies to them, they tune you out.

What Goes on in Your Listener's Mind?

1. **"Are you talking to me?"** Effective commercials identify the customers clearly.
   - "Do you have a car to sell?"
   - "Looking for lakefront properties?"

Because people are doing something else while listening to the radio, in order to get their attention, your message must address their needs. A proven method is to ask a question - a short, precise question. Questions are an important part of human communication. Questions evoke answers and get people thinking. Many everyday conversations begin with a question; and radio is just like a friend asking another friend if he needs something. Some advertising people object to asking questions because it's not "creative," and the listeners may say "no." Look! You are not trying to win awards; you are trying to *mass sell*. The goal is to qualify the listeners and sell to those who say "yes."

2. **"What's in it for me?"** To look out for oneself is human. The most successful radio commercials appeal to this very instinct.

   Maxwell Sackheim wrote, "Sell the results of the product, not the product itself." The promise of a benefit gives the listener a reason to buy. In fact, Samuel Johnson said, "Promise, large promise, is the soul of an advertisement." This is the reason why listeners are willing to drop everything they're doing to respond to a radio commercial, even though they consider commercials a nuisance. Listeners usually decide within 10 seconds whether to tune out of a selling message. So make known the benefit early.

3. **"Who are you anyway?"** Identify your brand early in the commercial, and repeat it often. Spell it out if it's an unusual name. For example, "…the solution to your problem is SkyMaxx…S-K-Y-M-A-X-X…"

In addition, consider voicing over your own commercials so that you speak directly to your listeners. People are more ready to buy from friends than from strangers. When you voice over your own commercials, you are building friendships over the air.

Alternatively, hire your radio station's most popular hosts to endorse your brand in order to tap into their following.

4. **"What makes you so special?"** If every commercial sounds the same, people get bored. If the offers are similar, people get confused. So, say something that your competitors have not said. Be the first to claim a category, or create your own category. Create a persona for your company. Dare to be different.

5. **"What are you trying to sell?"** Bad commercials leave the listeners wondering what is being sold. Stick with one simple offer and repeat it. Simplicity works best on the radio. Your listeners should be able to grab your meaning in a flash.

6. **"What do I have to lose?"** People like to win and hate to lose. They may be tempted by your offer but afraid to take it for fear of being taken in. Reassurances such as "free estimate" and "money-back guarantee" will motivate responses.

7. **"What do you want me to do?"** Effective radio commercials motivate listeners to take action. Ask for their business, and give your listeners clear instructions on how to respond to your offer. Do you want them to call? Visit your store? Log on to your web site? Do not leave them wondering.

8. **"How do I find you?"** Make it easy for your customers to find you. Addresses are impossible to remember, so don't bother to say them on the radio. If you want people to visit your store, refer to landmarks and cross roads. Say the city first. Then repeat the intersection. For example,

- "Visit our Miami showroom...on 75th and Lincoln. That's 75th and Lincoln."

- "We're in Kingsville...on Route 30, two miles East of I61. That's Route 30, East of I61."

If you want to give your web address, say it *twice in a row*. If your web address contains a difficult or uncommon word, spell it out for the listeners.

If you want people to call, you must end your commercial with your phone number; not a word should follow it. The last thing you say will reverberate in the minds of the listeners for a few good seconds. Repeat your phone number *three times in a row at dictation speed.* For example,

- If your phone number were 800-552-2020, say this: "Call now! Eight hundred, five five two, twenty twenty. Eight hundred, five five two, twenty twenty. That's eight hundred, five five two, twenty twenty."

- If your phone number were 212-899-1616, say this: "Call now! Two one two, eight nine nine, sixteen sixteen. Two one two, eight nine nine, sixteen sixteen. *That's eight nine nine*, sixteen sixteen."

Other Factors that Affect The Effectiveness of Your Radio Commercial

Delivery / Announcement

How radio copy is voiced-over affects the response that it generates. Radio commercials should sound conversational and believable. The announcer should sound as if he were talking to a friend; he should not sound like he is reading a script.

Disclaimers / Legal Qualifiers

If your offer carries a disclaimer (e.g., "A Residential Mortgage Licensee," "Equal Opportunity Housing"), you should weave it into the copy whenever the law allows. Try not to end a radio commercial with a disclaimer, as it will weaken the response. Your contact information (phone number, web address or the company name) should be the last thing your listeners hear if you want direct response.

If your offer requires a *long* disclaimer, you should reconsider making that offer on radio altogether. Since there's no way to show fine print on radio, the only way to fulfill the legal requirements is to read them very fast. That's why we often hear fast-talking gibberish on radio; and we wonder what the advertiser is trying to hide by talking so fast! Fast reading of disclaimers creates suspicion in the minds of the listeners and destroys your offer.

Dramatization

You don't have to create a mini soap opera to sell something. Simply narrate a good story. The listeners will see the drama in their minds.

If you must include dramatization, it is worth hiring actors to do it professionally. Otherwise, your commercials could sound like a high school drama class project.

Humor

Stay away from humorous copy. It is extremely difficult to get humor to work in a commercial. Even if it works, it goes stale fast, and you'll have to produce another commercial. In many cases, the listeners remember the jokes but not the products being advertised.

Jingles

Jingles are a time-tested technique in radio advertising. A good jingle can stay in the memory of the listeners for years! However, jingles are not do-it-yourself projects. You should hire a production house that specializes in jingles, using trained musicians, experienced writers and professional singers in the production. There's no room for experiments. Once you've used a jingle, you're stuck with it.

Effective jingles are short and catchy. Never sing the entire commercial. David Ogilvy once said, "If you have nothing to sell, sing it." Keep your jingle simple. Sing only the brand name and maybe also the benefit.

Jingles need to be repeated frequently to be effective. A jingle that's heard once in a while has no impact.

Keeping the Winners

David Ogilvy reminded us, "If you are lucky enough to write a good advertisement, repeat it until it stops pulling." As long as your commercial is generating results, let it run. Too often, effective commercials are taken off the air simply because the advertisers get tired of them.

You don't have to re-invent the wheel to keep your commercial fresh. Rephrasing the copy, re-recording the commercial or using a different announcer often does the trick.

Length of Commercial

Although 60-second spots are widely used, the length of your commercial should depend on what you have to say. To orally communicate a sequence of ideas takes time. The more complex your ideas, the more time you need to explain them. Bear in mind, however, that listeners do not tune to a station to listen to long-winded commercials. Simplicity is an aid to brevity. Your goal is to say what you need to say in as little time as possible. For example, if a well-known store is having a sale, then 10 to 15 seconds is all it needs to publicize the sale.

Negative Selling

A good company does not need to denigrate others to stay on top. Negative selling almost always backfires, hurting not only your competitors but also your own business. It brings a bad reputation to your entire industry.

Sex

Does sex sell? That is debatable. However, one thing is obvious: sex cheapens the brand. The use of sexual references must be carefully calculated. It depends on the format of a station. It also depends on what industry the advertiser is in and how that business wants to be perceived.

The One Thing That
Your Listener Must Remember

One day, a listener called my station asking for the phone number of an advertiser. He had heard a commercial that offered something he needed badly. However, he could not remember the name of the advertiser. The problem was that there were two competitors advertising the same product on my station. I had no choice but to give him the phone numbers of *both* advertisers.

The moral of this story is that **if your listener remembers only one thing in your commercial, let it be your business name.** You can have the most attractive offer, the most creative commercial and the funniest joke, but if your listener does not remember your name, you are advertising for your competitors. The rule of thumb is to repeat your business name 4 to 6 times in a 60-second commercial.

Chapter 7

Radio: Your Ultimate Salesperson

Chapter 7

Radio: Your Ultimate Salesperson

How much do you pay your salespeople? $50,000 a year? $75,000? $125,000?

Instead of hiring a salesperson, hire radio to sell for you.

Here's why.

Suppose you pay your salesperson $50,000 a year plus benefits, and your salesperson makes 200 cold calls every single day.

> 200 cold calls per day x 5 work days
> = 1,000 cold calls per week
>
> 1,000 cold calls per week x 52 weeks
> = 52,000 cold calls a year

52,000 cold calls are all that your salesperson could make in an entire year! Of course, this example is extreme because it does not allow for any vacations or sick days.

Radio enables you to sell far more efficiently. Instead of talking to one person at a time, you talk to hundreds of thousands all at once. And you get to reach them over and over again.

This is the reason why so many of my clients advertise on radio. They could spend $50,000 on a salesperson and make only 52,000 cold calls a year, but they prefer to advertise on my station and reach a million people *several times over* for the same amount of money. Their employees would have to work 60 years to accomplish the feat, costing my clients millions of dollars in salaries and benefits!

If you are responsible for generating sales for your company, you should use your own voice on the radio to mass-sell. By doing so, it's as if you had hired your own clone, and your clone is turning cold leads into hot prospects so that you can focus on closing sales.

Chapter 8

Effective Scheduling

Chapter 8

Effective Scheduling

One day, a business owner emailed me that he would like to try radio advertising.

"Great!" I thought - until I read *how* he wanted to try it.

"I want to buy a couple of commercials in your prime time and see what happens," he wrote.

I declined his business. I didn't want him to become a casualty of bad scheduling. It would not be fair to him or to my station.

What is Effective Scheduling?

An effective schedule is one that produces enough results to justify the investment. After all, what's the point of adverting if it doesn't even pay for itself?

So now the question is: How many commercials do you need? 10? 100? Also, how long should your campaign last? 3 weeks? 3 months?

There is no one correct answer. It depends on a number of factors: whether your offer is unique; whether there is a demand for your product or service; whether you have competition; and whether you have the right message. Generally speaking, when it comes to effective radio advertising, there are nine rules to follow.

9 Rules of Effective Scheduling

1. Choose the right audience. Advertising to the wrong audience is a waste of money.

2. If a station runs long commercial breaks (i.e., 3 minutes or longer), make sure your commercial is the first to air. It makes no sense to buy 100 commercials only to have them stuck in long commercial breaks when most listeners have tuned out.

3. If you have a small budget, avoid buying the most expensive dayparts because they make it cost-prohibitive to build frequency.

4. In every effective schedule, there is saturation. Seek to dominate certain times of the day and days of the week. Make sure you achieve frequency before you worry about reach. Oral messages must be repeated to be memorable.

5. As soon as you have achieved a reasonable amount of frequency, you must expand your reach. Over-repeating

your message to the same listeners is a waste of money. Here's the rule of thumb: Of every 10 dollars you have, invest your first 3 dollars in frequency; pour your last 7 into reach. For example, many of my clients allocate 30% of their budget to weekends and evenings so that they dominate those dayparts. The remaining 70% of their budget is then spent on primetimes to build reach. Had they invested 100% of their money into primetimes, they would have reached a lot of people infrequently.

6. If your product or service has a long selling cycle, your radio advertising should span that entire period of time, if not longer. For example, if it takes you 3 months to close a sale, your radio campaign should last at least 3 months. And if you plan to stay in business for the next 20 years, you'd better keep advertising all this time.

7. Judge a station's proposal on its frequency and reach, not on the cost per spot.

8. The Gross Rating Point (GRP) and Cost per Point (CPP) are TV terms, and, therefore, irrelevant to radio and misleading to you as an advertiser. Judge a radio schedule by its frequency and

reach, never by GRP and CPP. (Refer to the next chapter for more discussion on this subject.)

9. The Cost per Thousand (CPM), however, is a much more reliable measurement of radio advertising efficiency than CPP. Since the CPM is also used to measure TV, newspapers, and magazines, it is useful when you're comparing the efficiency of different media.

Even if you know a radio station well, you should still seek the help of an experienced Account Executive when putting together an advertising schedule. That's because he knows his station better than you, and has the tools to calculate frequency, reach and CPM. Your job is to evaluate the proposal.

Chapter 8 ½

Persistence Pays Dividends

(Author Unknown)

The first time a man looks at an advertisement, he does not see it.

The second time, he does not notice it.

The third time, he is conscious of its existence.

The fourth time, he faintly remembers having seen it before.

The fifth time, he reads it.

The sixth time, he turns up his nose at it.

The seventh time, he reads it through and says, 'Oh brother!'

The eighth time, he says, 'Here's that confounded thing again!'

The ninth time, he wonders if it amounts to anything.

The tenth time, he asks his neighbor if he has tried it.

The eleventh time, he wonders how the advertiser makes it pay.

The twelfth time, he thinks it must be a good thing.

The thirteenth time, he thinks perhaps it might be worth something.

The fourteenth time, he remembers wanting such a thing a long time.

The fifteenth time, he is tantalized because he cannot afford to buy it.

The sixteenth time, he thinks he will buy it some day.

The seventeenth time, he makes a memorandum to buy it.

The eighteenth time, he swears at his poverty.

The nineteenth time, he counts his money carefully.

The twentieth time he sees the ad, he buys what it is offering.

Chapter 9

Basic Media Math

Chapter 9

Basic Media Math

By now you have come across a number of radio terms. In fact, you may have been using them when talking with your Account Executives. While you are not expected to know all the terms, you should know the basic ones. For example, you should know the difference between cume and AQH Persons; CPP and CPM. If your advertising has a frequency of 7, do you know what that means?

Who Measures Radio Audience?

Arbitron

When it comes to radio audience measurement, Arbitron dominates the arena. Arbitron is an independent research company whose ratings shape the fate of the $21 billion that is spent on radio advertising in the United States.

Arbitron collects information by having participants fill out diaries for a week, noting the radio stations that they listen to and the time of their listening. Arbitron then uses this information to create *quantitative* profiles of radio stations, and ranks them according to cume, AQH Persons, share…etc.

Scarborough

While Arbitron provides *quantitative* profiles, Scarborough provides *qualitative* ones.

Scarborough, a joint venture of Arbitron and VNU, ranks radio stations according to their listeners' life style, age, income, education, employment...etc. To collect such information, Scarborough conducts phone interviews and has participants fill out a Consumer Survey Booklet.

Media Audit

Media Audit is another research company whose data are often referenced by radio stations and advertising agencies. Media Audit collects audience data through phone interviews. Its participants do not fill out any diaries or questionnaires.

The Mumbo Jumbo

Dayparts

Radio programming is divided into blocks of time called dayparts. Each station has a different set of dayparts. In general, people speak of the following:

- Morning Drive: Monday - Friday, 6 AM - 10 AM (In major markets such as New

York, Los Angeles and Chicago, the Morning Drive may start at 5 AM on large stations.)
- Midday: Monday - Friday, 10 AM - 3 PM
- Afternoon Drive: Monday - Friday, 3 PM - 7 PM (In major markets, the Afternoon Drive may end at 8 PM on large stations.)

AQH Persons

The AQH Persons, Average-Quarter-Hour Persons, refers to **the average number of listeners a station reaches in a 15-minute period.** In plain English, it tells you how many people, on average, are listening to a station within any given 15 minutes.

The AQH Persons is a non-exclusive number, meaning that the same listeners may be counted over and over again in every quarter hour. Whenever you see a station with a lot of AQH Persons, you know that its listeners stay tuned for a long time. Advertising on such a station will enable you to build frequency quickly, but you will also run out of listeners quickly. Make sure that you do not over-repeat your commercials to the same audience. You need to add new stations to increase your reach.

Cume

Cume is the abbreviation for Cumulative Persons, **the number of unique listeners a radio station reaches**. In radio talk, cume is interchangeable with the term "reach." The station with the largest cume reaches the most people.

However, what cume does not tell you is how long those people listen. Whether a listener spends 5 minutes or 5 hours with a station, he is counted as one listener. Advertising on a station with a high cume enables you to reach many people. However, high-cuming stations tend to have fewer AQH Persons. For example, many All-News stations start to repeat themselves after 30 minutes. A listener may leave after catching what he needs, but the same listener will come back a few hours later to catch more news.

A cost-effective way to advertise on a high-cuming station is to buy a Total Audience Plan. Such a plan places your commercials in all dayparts so that the listener who hears you during the day will hear you again at night and on weekends when he tunes in again.

Rating

A rating is a percentage. The AQH Persons and the cume are often expressed as ratings.

- AQH rating: If there are 100,000 homeowners in a survey area, and 1,500 of them are listening to a particular radio station in any 15-minute interval, then that station has a 1.5% AQH rating among homeowners, or "a rating of one point five" or "one and a half rating points."

- Cume rating: If there are 100,000 homeowners in a survey area, and 10,000 of them listen to a particular station, then that station has a 10% cume rating among homeowners, or "a cume rating of ten."

GRP & CPP

The GRP and CPP are two TV measurements that work well for TV but break down when applied to radio. However, due to their prevalent use (and blind reliance) by many advertising agencies, we will discuss them here.

The GRP, Gross Rating Point, is the sum of all rating points delivered by an advertising schedule. For example, if a radio show has a rating of 2 (meaning 2% of the population is listening in any 15-minute interval), and if you run 5 spots on that show each week for 20 weeks, then the schedule will have 200 GRPs.

2 rating points x 5 spots x 20 weeks = 200 GRPs

The CPP, Cost Per Point, refers to the cost of each rating point. In this case, if you spend a total of $40,000, then your advertising will have a CPP of $200.

$40,000 ÷ 200 GRPs = $200

The Collapse of GRPs
When Imposed on Radio

Wow! 200 GRPs! A clear number for TV but a misleading one for radio. Here's why. TV viewers are loyal to the programs, not to the stations. They tune from one channel to another to watch their favorite shows. Over the course of a week, almost all TV households will have tuned to a particular station. As a result, it is possible to buy 200 GRPs on a single TV station and reach a high percentage of all TV households.

The same cannot be said about radio. That's because each listener sticks with only 2 to 3 stations. Most radio stations reach only a fraction of the total population. 200 GRPs on a single radio station would yield a disproportionately low reach and high frequency.

GRPs do not explain how many listeners are reached and at what frequency. 200 GRPs on radio could mean an infinite number of things:

- Reaching 10% of the population 20 times;
- Reaching 2% of the population 100 times;
- Reaching 0.5% of the population 400 times!!!

Judge a radio schedule on how many people will hear your commercial (reach) and how many times they will hear it (frequency).

Frequency

Frequency refers to the average number of times a listener hears a commercial. For example, if Listener A hears your commercial 10 times, Listener B 7 times, and Listener C 4 times, your advertising has an average frequency of 7 - or in radio talk, a frequency of 7.

$$(10 + 7 + 4) \div 3 = 7$$

Reach

Reach refers to the number of listeners who hear a commercial at least once. (When applied to a radio station, reach is synonymous with cume. For example, a station with a weekly cume of 1.2 million reaches 1.2 million listeners in a week.)

If 10 people hear your commercial once, you have a reach of 10. If those 10 listeners hear your commercial 50 times each, you still have a reach of 10.

CPM

The CPM, Cost Per Thousand, is a measurement of cost efficiency in advertising. The "M" is the Roman numeral for 1,000. Simply, CPM tells you how much it costs to reach 1,000 people *once*.

It is easy to calculate CPM. If you spend $500 and 50,000 people hear your commercial *once*, your CPM is $10:

$$\frac{\$500}{50,000 \text{ people} \times 1 \text{ time}} \times 1,000 = \$10$$

However, if you spend $500 and 50,000 people hear your commercial *ten times*, then your CPM will only be $1.

$$\frac{\$500}{50,000 \text{ people} \times 10 \text{ times}} \times 1,000 = \$1$$

In other words, it costs you only $1 to reach 1,000 people once.

Since the CPM is also used to measure advertising efficiency in other media (TV, direct mail, newspapers and magazines), it is especially useful when you make comparisons. Unlike the CPP which is based on averages and percentages, the CPM is based on reach and frequency - the building blocks of a solid radio schedule.

Chapter 10

How to Get the Most Out of Your Account Executive

Chapter 10

How to Get the Most Out of Your Account Executive

The job of an Account Executive is to facilitate your campaign. He is the link between your business and his radio station. His competence will directly affect your campaign. So make sure you get to know this person.

How Account Executives Are Paid

Account Executives are commissioned salespeople. Depending on the stations and markets, they may be paid anything from 3% to 20% of your advertising spending. Usually, large stations pay the lowest percentages and small stations, the highest. That's because large stations get larger billings. 3% on a $500,000 campaign is more income to the Account Executive than 20% on a $10,000 campaign.

Their being commissioned means a few things to you:

1. They don't get paid unless you advertise.
2. In an attempt to win your business, they invest a lot of time and effort into their proposals to you.

3. The rise or fall of their income depends on the success or failure of your advertising.
4. If you reduce your advertising, you reduce their income.
5. If you stop advertising, they stop getting paid.
6. Although Account Executives are employees of their stations, in effect, they work for you because their income comes from you.
7. Their pay structure makes them your advocates. They're on your side.
8. Their pay structure makes them entrepreneurs.

What to Look for in an Account Executive

If you've found a good Account Executive, take good care of him, for he is an asset to your business. If your Account Executive possesses the following qualities, you have found a gem.

1. He understands radio.
2. He knows his station well.
3. He understands your business.
4. He cares about your best interests, not his station's, nor his own.
5. He has business acumen.
6. He is a listener.
7. He is a thinker.

8. He is a writer.
9. He is a learner.
10. He is a good communicator.
11. He is enthusiastic.
12. He is a problem solver.
13. He is intelligent.
14. He is confident yet humble.
15. He is professional.
16. He projects integrity.
17. He believes in what he sells.
18. He is an advisor and a resource to you.
19. He keeps his promises.
20. He makes things happen.
21. He has many other clients.
22. He refers business to you.
23. He brings you good offers from his station.
24. He invites you to station events.
25. You wish that your employees were like him.

If you want to get the most out of your Account Executive, treat him as if he were a member of your staff. Show him appreciation as you would to any good employee. Involve him in your business. Invite him to your company events. In radio advertising, many contracts are never signed. They are agreed to with a hand shake between the Account Executive and the advertiser. The Account Executive knows the trade secrets of his clients. The level of trust between the two parties is remarkable! Not surprisingly, many radio Account Executives become life-long friends to their clients!

Leo Burnett once said, "I have learned that you can't have good advertising without a good client, and that you can't keep a good client without good advertising." If your Account Executive is doing a good job for you, you in turns need to be a good client to him.

Chapter 11

When to Hire an Advertising Agency

Chapter 11

When to Hire an Advertising Agency

I work at a top-10 station in a top-10 market. As a result, I get to work with some of the best advertising agencies in the business - "best" in terms of their understanding of radio, their knowledge of their clients' businesses, their ideas, and their relationships with their stations.

I also get to work with some of the most successful *direct advertisers* - those who do not use an advertising agency. Some of my station's direct clients have been with us for 10 years; a few even 20 years! And they have always done everything themselves. They write their own copy, voice over their own commercials, and book their own advertising. So what makes one advertiser use an agency and another, not? At what point should you hire an advertising agency to handle your radio campaign?

Characteristics of Direct Advertisers

Direct advertisers are very involved in the creative process of their advertising. Not surprisingly, many of them voice over their own commercials. The more well-known these business owners are, the more business they capture. They are local businesses. Many call themselves "small businesses," "family businesses," or "mom-and-pop shops" even though they may generate multi-million dollar revenues.

They advertise on one to three stations, rarely more. They often listen to the stations that they advertise with. They have close relationships with their stations. They play golf with station managers and attend station events. Most important, they have capable Account Executives who super-serve them.

Characteristics of Advertisers Who Use An Agency

Advertisers who let an advertising agency handle their radio campaigns fall into these categories.

1. They need customized, independent research.
2. They need help with planning and budgeting.
3. They advertise on multiple radio stations.
4. They advertise in multiple markets.
5. They do not have time to meet with account executives, to negotiate rates, to review invoices and to measure effectiveness.
6. They do not have time to write copy and voice over commercials.

7. They want creative, professionally-produced commercials.
8. They do not know anybody at the stations and have no time to get to know them.
9. They want to tap into their agencies' relationships with the stations to get good rates, upgrades and added value.

What to Look for in an Adverting Agency

Not all advertising agencies know how to buy radio advertising. The fact that there is still a blind reliance on CPP among advertising agencies despite the protest from the radio industry is troubling. When searching for an advertising agency to help with your radio campaign, look for the following qualifications and qualities.

1. The agency knows the difference between effective advertising and clever advertising, and prides itself on the former.
2. The agency understands your business.
3. The agency is well-rounded. Its experience includes radio buying and production.
4. The agency comes up with better ideas than you.
5. The agency has *long-running* campaigns on radio.

6. The agency meets with account executives regularly and reviews new offers.
7. The agency's relationships with the radio stations go beyond the account executives' level.
8. The agency has established credit with the finance departments of these radio stations.
9. The agency negotiates better deals than you by using the leverage of its large volume of business.

Chapter 12

Advertising & Promotion Laws

Chapter 12

Advertising & Promotion Laws

Advertising is regulated by both federal and state laws. The Federal Trade Commission (FTC) regulates national advertising. Local matters are handled by local authorities such as the states' Attorney Generals, as well as by trade organizations such as the Better Business Bureaus.

Although radio is a local medium, when you advertise on stations in different states, your campaign becomes both local and national, and falls under both jurisdictions.

Whether advertising locally or nationally, you must comply with the Truth-in-Advertising Rules set by the FTC Act.

- **Your advertising must be truthful and non-deceptive.** (If reasonable consumers are misled because of what your commercial says or omits, you are guilty of deceptive advertising.)

- **You must have evidence to back up your claims.** (You must have proof to substantiate both *expressed* and *implied* claims.)

111

- **You cannot be unfair.** (If reasonable consumers suffer substantial injuries - be they physical, mental or financial - as a result of responding to your commercial, you have advertised unfairly.)

Legal Matters That Concern Radio Advertising

Bait and Switch

It is illegal to advertise a product that you have no intention of selling, using it just as a bait for the consumers to whom you wish to sell something else.

Consumer Credit

The Truth in Lending Act requires the disclosure of consumer credit and lease terms. If you offer credit or lease, you must comply with the law. According to the FTC, "the more specific the statement, the more likely it is to trigger additional disclosures." Here are some of the examples listed on the FTC's web site:

Disclosures Needed (The mention of a number)	No Disclosures Needed (General statements)
<ul><li>"10% down"</li><li>"90% financing"</li><li>"$210.95 per month"</li><li>"48 months to pay"</li><li>"30-year mortgages available"</li><li>"Less than $1,200 interest"</li></ul>	<ul><li>"No down payment"</li><li>"Easy monthly payments"</li><li>"Pay weekly"</li><li>"Terms to fit your budget"</li><li>"Financing available"</li></ul>

Although radio stations are not held liable under the Truth in Lending Act, they owe it to their listeners to ensure that advertisers comply with the law.

Contests and Prize Promotions

Contests are a fun way for radio stations to interact with listeners, and for sponsors to build name recognition and goodwill. However, radio stations and sponsors must be aware that promotions that require a purchase are *illegal* in the United States. In many cases, you are required to disclose "the odds on winning a prize, how to participate without buying anything, and that no purchase or payment is required to win."

In fact, contests and prize promotions encompass a variety of rules and regulations enforced by different federal and local agencies, including the FTC, the United States Postal Service (USPS) and the Federal Communications Commission (FCC), as well as the states' Attorneys General.

Dietary Supplements

Claims for dietary supplements must be truthful and substantiated by evidence. The advertiser is responsible for both expressed and implied claims. For example, if your commercial claims that most cancer specialists use your dietary supplement, not only must you produce proof that most cancer specialists indeed use your product (expressed claim) but also that your product has cancer-fighting benefits (implied claim).

Disclosures and Disclaimers

The FTC requires prominent disclosures and disclaimers in certain types of advertising such as consumer leases, credit and 1-900 telephone numbers. In addition, local governments have their own requirements. In Illinois, for example, a mortgage company must inform the public that it is an "Illinois Residential Mortgage Licensee."

Disclosures and disclaimers must be *clearly and conspicuously* communicated to the consumers. Although there is no hard-and-fast rule about the speed at which a disclosure or disclaimer may be announced on radio, the FTC and local authorities can take action against an advertiser whose disclosure or disclaimer is read too fast, buried in other information, or otherwise hard for listeners to comprehend.

Endorsements and Testimonials

Endorsements and testimonials by consumers, celebrities, and experts must reflect their honest experience or opinion. Their claims must be substantiated.

- **Consumer Testimonials**: Such testimonials must reflect the *typical* experience of all consumers, not the experience of a few happy customers. Otherwise, the commercial must disclose either what a typical consumer *can* expect, or the limited applicability of the endorsers' experience. Saying "Results may vary" is not enough. Also, an advertiser must disclose if the consumers have been paid for endorsing the product.

- **Celebrity Endorsements**: Such endorsements must reflect the celebrity's true experience or opinion. If the

115

celebrity claims that he uses the product, he must use the product.

- **Expert Endorsement:** A person must have sufficient qualifications to give an expert endorsement. In addition, his endorsement must be "supported by an actual evaluation, examination, or testing of the product."

"Free" Offers

When you make a "free" offer, you must not increase the price of the product that this free offer is tied to. For example, if you offer a free refrigerator for every kitchen remodeling project, you must not increase the price of the remodeling project to cover the cost of the refrigerator.

"Going Out Of Business Sale"

It is illegal to advertise a "Going Out Of Business Sale" when a business is *not* going out of business.

Liabilities of Advertising Agencies

Advertising agencies are also subject to the FTC Act and can be held legally liable for deceptive claims made in their clients' commercials. After all, it is part of an advertising agency's duty to verify its clients' claims. The agency must not rely on its clients' assertion that the claims are substantiated.

Liabilities of Radio Stations

Although media outlets are generally not held liable in cases of deceptive advertising, they are not automatically exculpated either. As FTC Commissioner Sheila F. Anthony pointed out, "the First Amendment does not protect fraud." The media's liabilities lie in the amount of involvement they have in the creation of false or harmful advertising.

Radio is in a unique position. Compared to TV, magazines and newspapers, radio is the most involved in the creation of their advertisers' commercials. From initiating the campaign idea to writing the copy to producing the commercial, a radio station can be the sole creative force behind a campaign, and therefore must be able to substantiate the claims that it helps write, produce and promote.

However, even when a radio station is not involved in the creation of a commercial message, if it has reason to believe that the message is deceptive or harmful to its listeners, the station owes it to its listeners to refuse to air it. It's a matter of integrity.

Weight Loss Products

The FTC, as well as the Attorneys General, has prosecuted advertisers who falsely promised easy weight loss. If you promote diet products or services, or make representations about "fat loss, weight loss, calorie burning, or the loss of inches or cellulite" you must substantiate your claims with scientific evidence.

Legal Information Is Not Legal Advice

This chapter has provided legal information about radio advertising. However, legal information is not the same as legal advice. It is not a full and exhaustive explanation; nor is it specific enough to be applicable to your unique situation. You must consult a lawyer if you need professional assurance that the information contained in this chapter and your interpretation of it are applicable to your particular situation.

For more information on advertising rules and regulations, please visit:

www.ftc.gov

Chapter 13

Play-by-Play Sports Radio: Theatre of the Mind Exemplified

Chapter 13

Play-by-Play Sports Radio: Theatre of the Mind Exemplified

Play-by-play is a broadcast term referring to the reporting of a sporting event with an announcer "calling the game," describing the details of the action so that the listeners get to see the images and feel the emotions. When the game is not in progress, a *color commentator* usually fills in with analyses, statistics and injury reports.

Theatre of the Mind Personified

The play-by-play broadcast is the perfect example of how radio triggers the theatre of the mind. Sports fans *watch* their games on radio; and they see it all by listening!

A Gold Mine for Advertisers

Play-by-play radio attracts large numbers of loyal fans. They come back game after game, season after season, listening attentively and faithfully. They are not "button-pushers;" they stay tuned through the commercials because they don't want to miss a moment of the game.

OK. Let's say this together: **A huge audience that listens attentively time after time, and doesn't tune out of commercials.**

Hello! All the marketers out there! Have your light bulbs lit up yet?

Play-by-play sports radio is, therefore, a golden opportunity for advertisers to **reach a large number of loyal listeners consistently.**

Benefits of Advertising on Play-by-Play Sports Radio

1. Branding

People won't buy what they don't know. Play-by-play sports radio can make your brand well-known by exposing it to the huge audience that tunes in to every game.

2. Abnormally high recall

We remember things by association. Our memory is even more vivid when it is associated with emotions. Sporting events are where emotions run high. It's no wonder that listeners recall brands advertised during the game.

Commercial Isolation and Brevity

Sporting events are action-packed. There is no time for long commercial breaks and long-winded sales pitches. As a result, you know that your commercial will stand out, and not be buried in clutter. By the same token, your commercial must fit into the fast-paced, action-packed environment; it too must be concise.

3. Credibility

If credibility is important to your business, then your association with the home team will add credibility to your name. On play-by-play radio, copy is often voiced over by a popular local announcer or even by a famous athlete, turning your name into a trusted brand in the community.

4. Networking

Advertisers on play-by-play sports radio get to enjoy the action from the comfort of a corporate suite. These advertisers often bring their own clients to the games to impress them. At the corporate suite, advertisers and their clients meet other advertisers and their clients, thereby forming a business networking session in the middle of a sporting event.

5. Promotions

Much of play-by-play radio's revenue comes from promotions. Your station may be able to get your products displayed, sampled and demonstrated at the stadium. Also, it can customize on-site contests for fans to participate in so that they may win prizes from you.

6. Player Appearances

Player appearances have filled business premises with hundreds, even thousands of people! Whether you want people to come to your grand opening, your sale, your new product launch, if you want a large number of people to come to your store, have your radio station arrange for a player appearance.

Play-by-Play Sports Radio is about Branding, Not Direct Response

One thing you must understand about advertising on play-by-play sports radio is that it does not generate direct response. You will not get immediate phone calls from commercials aired during the sportscast. That's because all the listeners are too busy *watching* the game on radio to respond to any commercial. However, they will remember your name and associate it with their favorite team!

Never judge your advertising on play-by-play sports radio by how many immediate calls you receive. The benefits of play-by-play radio are intangible. Credibility, prestige, good will, loyalty, brand awareness and confidence cannot be measured by the number of phone calls.

Chapter 14

10 Sins in Radio Advertising

Chapter 14

10 Sins in Radio Advertising

1. Not Taking Advantage of Radio's Strengths

Many advertisers and advertising agencies that have been successful with other media think that they also know radio. They impose on radio the same criteria used in other media and fail miserably.

Here are the correct principles. Use print to display details but use radio to establish top-of-mind awareness. Use coupons to make quick sales but use radio to develop long-term loyalty. Advertise in the Yellow Pages so that your customers can find you, but advertise on radio to find your customers. Use TV to demonstrate before one's eyes but use radio to paint pictures in one's mind. Apply GRP to TV but reach and frequency to radio.

2. Lacking Marketability

Before you advertise on radio, make sure that your business is marketable on radio. Do you have a unique selling proposition? Do you have a specific offer? Is your offer compelling? Do you or does your company have a certain

129

persona? Are your phone number and web address easy to announce?

Difficult to Announce	Easy to Announce
213-502-0190	213-BUY-MORE
866-146-7283	800-CAR-2000
Radio-4me.biz	RadioAdvertisingBook.com

3. Over-Reliance on Ratings

Time and time again, lower-rated stations outperform higher-rated ones in generating phone calls and store traffic. Ratings are estimates. They serve as references, not absolute truths. Mathematical errors occur when estimated numbers are added up and then averaged out, and this averaged number is then turned into a percentage and further rounded off. Now, how reliable can the final number be? Are you sure you want to base your radio buy on such a number? Why not just go back to the basic principle of radio advertising? That is: repeat a good offer to a large number of potential customers.

4. Over-Emphasis on Drive Times

Many advertisers and media buyers have the misconception that a successful radio campaign must include drive times. Not only is this belief wrong but also costly! Radio rates are driven by demand. As advertisers compete for drive times, they push the high price higher still. Each time they buy drive times, they are paying a premium, thereby increasing their cost per sale and lowering their profit margins. These advertisers end up paying an inflated price, reaching a lot of people at a reduced frequency. This totally goes against the logic of radio advertising.

5. Bad Copy, Bad Production

Saying too much, too fast. Failing to stress the benefits. Bragging about himself by the business owner. Failing to repeat the brand name. Lacking a strong call to action. Failing to create a sense of urgency. Bashing the competition. Not ending the commercial with a phone number in a direct-response message. Not repeating the phone number. Singing the entire sales pitch. Making unfunny jokes. Using boring dialogue. Economizing with an amateurish production. All are sins.

6. Choosing a Station Based on Cost

Radio stations are treated as if they were commodities the only difference between which is price. The truth is that good stations are not cheap; cheap stations are not good. Furthermore, each station has its own unique audience so that advertising on one station means missing the audience of another. One should choose a station because it delivers the right audience and has a track record of producing results, not because its spot rates are low.

7. Choosing a Station Based on GRP and CPP

If one radio station runs only 2 commercials per break and employs credible announcers, and another station runs 6 commercials in each break and features unknown hosts, then the station that has less clutter and more credibility will generate better results for its advertisers.

Yet when the decision to purchase is based on GRP and CPP, the poorer station can look better on paper because ratings do not measure "commercial load" and "credibility." Is it fair to the better station? Is it fair to yourself?

8. Over-Reliance on What Customers Say Brought Them In

Most people don't know how they heard about you and what brought them into your store. Before a customer walks in, a series of events may have happened. He may have seen your newspaper advertisements a few months earlier, spoken with his wife about the possible purchase, researched your products on your web site, received a coupon from you by mail and heard you on the radio that very day inviting him to your store. What brought him in? ALL of your advertising brought him in. Your newspaper featured the product; your web site educated him about it; your coupon gave him an incentive; and your radio commercial motivated him to take action.

9. "Let's Run A Few Spots and See What Happens"

When you're flying an airplane, would you say to yourself, "Let's switch off the engine and see what happens?"

When you're baking a cake, would you say to yourself, "Let's turn off the oven and see what happens?"

10. Making False Claims to Listeners

This is the ultimate sin in radio. In fact, it is the ultimate sin in advertising. To abuse the trust of the public is unforgivable.

Chapter 15

5 Things That Radio Cannot Do

Chapter 15

5 Things That Radio Cannot Do

Radio when used properly can help you promote virtually any product and service. However, there are five things that you should not expect radio (or any other medium for that matter) to do.

1. **Radio cannot guarantee sales.**

   Radio generates inquiries, motivates purchases and shortens your selling cycle. Ultimately it is you and your salespeople who will turn leads into customers.

2. **Radio cannot substitute for superb customer service.**

   Radio initiates goodwill, but it is your superb customer service that will sustain it.

3. **Radio cannot create an immediate customer base**

   Radio brings you a sudden increase in inquiries, but not in immediate sales. However motivated, people still need time to complete a purchase. However well-known and trusted, a company still needs to spend the time and effort to earn its business.

4. Radio cannot solve problems inherent in a company.

Radio can solve marketing problems but not problems caused by poor management, poor cash flow, poor planning, and poor staffing within a company.

5. Radio cannot sell something that people no longer want.

Popular products of the past are constantly phased out by new products. Typewriters have been replaced by computers; film is being phased out by digital photography; dial-up Internet by high-speed wireless Internet. No amount of radio advertising can bring back the glories of the past.

Chapter 16

The Future of Radio

Chapter 16

The Future of Radio

Are you ready for the biggest revolution in radio broadcasting? The radio of tomorrow will be drastically different from the radio we know today, thanks to High Definition (HD) radio.

What Is HD Radio

HD radio is digital radio. HD technology enables AM and FM stations to broadcast digitally – the most significant advancement in radio broadcasting since the introduction of FM stereo.

In fact, HD radio is already here! As of April 2006, hundreds of stations across the United States are already transmitting digital signals alongside their analog ones to give consumers time to adopt the new technology.

HD radio offers amazing improvements.

- AM stations sound like FM.
- FM stations sound like CDs.
- The signal is crystal-clear. Fades, static and hiss are out; surround sound is in!
- The names of DJs, artists and songs, as well as contact information of

advertisers can be displayed on the screen of an HD radio receiver.

- Real-time traffic updates can be displayed on a navigation map.
- Stations multicast different programs simultaneously, offering more choices to listeners.
- Listeners can store a radio program for later replay.
- Listeners can download songs and purchase products with the push of a button.

HD radio will revolutionize the way listeners use radio, making this pervasive, portable, personal medium even more so! And the best thing is: HD radio is *free*!

Implications of HD Radio for Advertisers

The implications of HD radio for advertisers are significant.

More Time Spent with Radio

With surround sound, deeper bass, higher treble, greater stereo separation, and a wider dynamic range, HD radio will greatly enhance the listening experience. Listeners who usually switch between radio and CDs will now have the incentive to stay tuned to radio.

In addition to the listening pleasure, listeners will have more programs to choose from, thanks to multicasting. HD radio technology allows as many as eight separate stations to be broadcast in the same spectrum currently allocated to a single station. For example, an all-news station can add a second channel dedicated to in-depth financial news; a third channel to political analyses; and a fourth channel to listeners' opinions.

The rich contents of HD radio will give listeners more reasons to listen longer and more often.

Niche Advertising in a Broad Medium

Radio has always been a highly targetable medium even without the multicasting. With HD technology, radio will reach even better-defined demographic and psychographic groups. This means that narrow-target advertisers will be able to take advantage of this medium more cost-efficiently.

The Ultimate Direct-Response Medium

HD technology will make radio the ultimate direct-response medium. Listeners will be able to see on the screens of their radio receivers the names and phone numbers of the advertisers. Moreover, HD radio has the capability to offer instant music downloads and product purchases. What better way for a listener to save time when stuck in traffic than to finish the week's grocery shopping and order grandma's birthday bouquet via HD radio?

More Choices, More Channel Surfing?

The answer is yes. With the increase in the number of radio stations, listeners will be more likely to tune away to avoid commercials. As a result, radio program directors need to keep their commercial breaks short; advertisers need to keep their commercials concise; and Account Executives need to do a better job matching the advertisers with the listeners.

In addition, the radio audience will be even more segmented. That means advertisers with a wide appeal need to be on multiple stations in order to reach a large percentage of the population.

The Same Principles Still Apply

The same principles that have worked on terrestrial radio will still apply to HD radio. In fact, those principles need to be adhered to even more stringently.

You will still be buying an audience. In fact, you will need to do an even better job at matching your customers' demographics with the station's. The listeners will still be asking "What's in it for me?" And you will still have to give a compelling answer. You will always have to repeat your name, phone number and web address, despite the visual displays on the radio receiver, because you still want to pound that information into your listeners' heads so they will in turn tell their friends about you. HD or not, radio will still be the word-of-mouth medium.

Chapter 17

A Few Recommendations for the Radio Industry

Chapter 17

A Few Recommendations for the Radio Industry

1. **Radio should hire well-rounded, accomplished people as Account Executives.**

   The radio industry hires very young, inexperienced people to sell air time when it should hire credible, entrepreneurial consultants to sell solutions. Not surprisingly, there's a high turnover rate among new Account Executives at every radio station. They simply do not have enough life experience nor mental toughness to handle the responsibilities that come with the job.

   There is not one personality type for good Account Executives. Some are extroverts; others, introverts. Some like to sell; others prefer to educate. But all are problem solvers and relationship builders.

   One way of finding good Account Executives is to train promising candidates internally. In the first year or two, the trainees should be sent to work in all departments (i.e., traffic, finance, production, sales, marketing and even engineering) where they can learn every aspect of the job. They are promoted to the level of Account Executive only after they have proved themselves worthy of the position. Incidentally, the friendships built during this period will be invaluable when they become Account Executives.

2. Radio must reduce clutter or it will lose listeners.

It is amazing that many radio stations continue to run commercial breaks as long as 10 minutes! Have they not heard of the iPod and satellite radio? Running more than 2 minutes of commercials is annoying to the listeners and unfair to the advertisers. Soon, listeners will be able to stream music from the Internet into their cell phones and into their vehicles. And with the launch of HD radio, listeners will have even more choices. They will not tolerate long commercial breaks.

3. Radio stations must stop speaking ill of one another.

Radio stations are notorious for bashing one another when fighting over a piece of business. The industry needs to show some class.

4. **Radio must invest in local DJs, hosts and personalities.**

Some stations seem to have forgotten why people tune to radio in the first place. People tune in because they need companionship. Listeners are usually alone. Alone in their cars. Alone at home. Alone but not lonely because they have for company that familiar voice on the radio.

Sadly, industry consolidations have taken away much of that human, intimate connection that radio has with its listeners. Now, many stations sound the same. Some do not even feature a live DJ. They play songs, commercials, more songs, and more commercials.

Other stations try to cheat with the aid of voice-tracking technology which allows them to use the same personalities in different cities. But listeners are smart. They can tell when a DJ is not local but is trying to sound like he is. When there are no strong local personalities, it is difficult for listeners to view their stations as "friends," let alone feel any loyalty towards them.

5. **Radio should help train new generations of media planners, buyers and copywriters.**

Radio is a $21 billion industry; more money is spent on radio advertising than on magazine advertising! Yet, there are few books written about radio advertising!

Despite its wide appeal, radio is the least taught and least researched by universities, and the most overlooked by advertisers and advertising agencies. Textbooks give the subject only cursory treatment. Most professors are not familiar with radio as an advertising medium. Degree programs at universities focus too much on the creation of commercials as art rather than on the eliciting of a direct response from the public. Most advertising agencies are ill-equipped in buying radio advertising.

It is time for the radio industry to reach out to the academic world to influence the training of those who intend to work in this medium.

To My Readers

April 2006

Dear Readers,

I hope that this book has helped you understand radio as an advertising medium, and that as a result of this book you become another success story in radio advertising.

Sincerely,

The Author

Volume discounts are available at

www.RadioAdvertisingBook.com